MAKE BRACELETS

16 Projects for Creating Beautiful Bracelets

Quarry Books
Rockport, Massachusetts
Distributed by North Light Books
Cincinnati, Ohio

capam 15.99

First published in the United States of America by
Quarry Books, an imprint of Rockport Publishers, Inc.
146 Granite Street
Rockport, Massachusetts 01966-1299
Telephone: (508) 546-9590
Fax: (508) 546-7141

Distributed to the book trade and art trade
in the United States of America by
North Light, an imprint of F & W Publications
1507 Dana Avenue
Cincinnati, Ohio 45207
Telephone: (800) 289-0963

Other distribution by
Rockport Publishers, Inc.
Rockport, Massachusetts 01966-1299

ISBN: 1-56496-272-5

10   9   8   7   6   5   4   3   2   1

Designer: Laura Herrmann Design

Printed in Hong Kong
by Regent Publishing Services Limited

CONTENTS

3

BRACELET BASICS

Y OU DON'T HAVE TO BE A HIGHLY SKILLED PROFESSIONAL TO CREATE beautiful bracelets that make you the envy of your friends. With just a little imagination and the right materials and tools, you can produce wonderful works of art from classic jewelry elements such as beads, precious metals, and stones. Or you can transform mundane, household items such as buttons, fabric scraps, and newspapers into sophisticated bracelets. To produce fabulous designs with a professional finish, you will need the findings, tools, and techniques that join, link, and make up your bracelet.

Materials

Beads have been used in jewelry making since the beginning of time, but they can be expensive to buy in large quantities. Many of the projects in this book show you how to make your own beads using materials such as modeling clay and paper. The clays can be twisted together in different color combinations to create wonderful marbled effects or built up into imitation millefiori canes—a technique used more often by glass workers. Papier-mâché beads can be painted to mimic ceramic beads or hand-decorated to make them look extra special. Strips of colorful paper can be rolled to make beads of different shapes and lengths. Pick up other materials at yard sales and antique fairs. Never throw out a broken necklace or bracelet—the remaining beads and clasps can always be worked into other designs.

Almost all jewelry making requires the use of *findings*, which is the jeweler's term for the basic components that connect the pieces of your bracelet and give it a neat finish. Findings help each piece hang correctly. They should be the right size for your bracelet; if they are in proportion to the materials that you choose for your bracelet, they will help balance the overall design.

Findings

JUMP RINGS are circular or oval metal rings that are not completely joined together. They come in a variety of sizes and thicknesses to suit all kinds of jewelry projects. Use them to link two findings together.

CLASPS usually consist of two pieces, attached to each end of the bracelet, that join together to secure it around your wrist. They come in an assortment of designs, including screw clasps, spring rings, barrel clasps, and S-clasps. You can also buy decorative two-part clasps that have preformed holes for more than one thread. These can be set with diamanté, pearls, or rhinestones. Choose a style that suits your bracelet design and that is easy to open and close with one hand.

HEAD PINS and EYE PINS are wire pins that come in various lengths to link beads to each other or to a bracelet chain. A head pin, which has a flat head at one end like a blunt dressmaker's pin, is particularly useful for making pendant drops and charms. Eye pins have a preformed loop at one end and are most often used to link together beads or findings.

Other Findings

Use JEWELER'S WIRE when head and eye pins are not long enough. It is available in gold and silver in many gauges and can be coiled into decorative spiral charms. The finer the gauge of wire, the easier it is to work with. Choose a wire thickness to suit the beads and the overall design of the bracelet, especially if it is a visible part of the design.

CALOTTE CRIMPS conceal and secure knots at both ends of a bracelet. They help make the finished piece look polished. Calotte crimps come in different sizes to suit the thread you are using and in slightly different styles; round calottes can open sideways or from the top; square calottes are ideal for thicker threads and for clamping unusual materials such as feathers.

Other findings to use when making jewelry are ornate SPACERS and HANGERS, which often have two, three, or five preformed holes. End SPACER BARS can be used to make multistrand designs and to attach the clasp to the start and finish of a bracelet. Incorporate more decorative spacer bars as part of the design itself. Large BELL CAPS are a decorative cap added to each end of a bracelet to conceal a collection of knots. Join pendant clasps to jump rings to make a pendant or charm hang correctly, or directly clamp on to fabric or seed charms.

The most important findings are jump rings, calotte crimps, head or eye pins, jeweler's wire, and clasps. These may all sound rather strange now but by the time you have worked through the projects in this book, they will be much more familiar to you. All findings are readily available in craft stores, from bead suppliers, and even in department stores. You can buy them in precious or nonprecious metals.

Tools & Adhesives

All of the projects in this book are easy to make and require little space for their creation—most can be put together at the kitchen table with only the basic tools. Lay down a craft board to protect the table from damage, and provide a flat, even surface to work on. Organize your beads and findings in boxes and trays.

Small round-nosed and needle-nosed pliers, available at jewelry and bead suppliers, make opening, closing, and linking together findings much easier. Use round-nosed pliers to turn loops, and to twist and coil wire into shape. Squeeze calotte crimps together and flatten

joints with needle-nosed pliers. Use two pairs of pliers to open and close jump rings. Buy them with integral wire cutters or invest in a separate pair of wire cutters for trimming head and eye pins, and jeweler's wire.

As a general rule, an all-purpose, clear-drying glue is all you will need to ensure that your wonderful design won't break when you wear it. Take the time to read and follow the directions on the glue container. Use common sense: make sure that bead and finding surfaces are clean and grease-free; and, with some glues, you may need to work in a well-ventilated room.

Stringing & Knotting

Stringing beads onto thread is the simplest way to make a bracelet. To determine the length of the bracelet, wrap a piece of cord or string around your wrist: for a charm bracelet, let the piece hang loosely without falling off your wrist; for a pull-on, pull-off, elasticized bracelet, it should fit snugly around your wrist. If you use shirring elastic for such bracelets, cut it a little shorter than your wrist measurement to let it stretch. Otherwise, to allow for knotting, add 3 inches / 7.5 cm to each side of the length of cord or string. To calculate the total number of beads you will need to make a bracelet, count how many beads fit into 1 inch / 2.5 cm, then multiply this by the length required. Select a thread and clasp suitable for the beads and the design. If the bracelet is threaded on elastic, it won't need a clasp; after stringing on all the beads, knot the two ends of the elastic together

and add a little glue to the knot, which can be concealed inside a bead. For more tailored bracelets, knot one end of the thread and secure it in a calotte crimp. String on the beads, knot the opposite end of the thread, and insert it in a calotte crimp again. The crimps have preformed rings that are easy to attach to a bracelet clasp with jump rings. (See *Finishing Techniques*).

The size and weight of the beads you choose determines which thread to use. Consider whether the thread will be visible, whether it will be strong enough to support the beads, and if it will fit through the holes in the beads. Silk and cotton thread both hang well and can be color-coordinated to the beads, but they are not very strong. Use several strands together if you are working with heavy beads. To prevent them from getting tangled, run them through a beeswax cake. Or try polyester thread already coated with beeswax. If you prefer the drape of the silk and cotton threads, knot between every bead or small group of beads to prevent the beads from tumbling in all directions if the thread breaks.

When making a bracelet with a central point of interest, work from the middle outward on both threads at the same time, keeping the design symmetrical. Another advantage of working from the center out is that the length can be adjusted by adding or taking away beads at each end.

Fine, invisible thread, though not very strong, is useful for stringing tiny lightweight beads like rocailles because it can be threaded through a beading needle. Nylon line and tiger tail are more substantial and will support most designs. They are both almost invisible to the eye and can be used without a needle. Nylon is inexpensive and easy to handle, but will not always hang well, so it is best for fun bead bracelets. Tiger tail is a good, all-purpose jeweler's thread. It is made from fine strands of steel cable in a plastic coating and is therefore very strong, but it does have a tendency to kink. It is easy to make starter

knots in tiger tail, though sometimes you need pliers to pull it tight, or you can make a loop and secure it with a crimp bead. Leather thong, decorative cord, string, and even raffia can also be used. Thong is good for stringing individual beads or small groups of beads or objects with large holes. String and raffia can be used to complement more unusual material, such as shells.

Most bracelets need a knot at both ends that can then be concealed by either a bead or by calotte crimps. Thicker threads and leather thong can be clamped directly into a calotte without knotting. Knots can also be used as decorative spacers or as a protective measure between beads, but as these must be large enough not to slip through the holes in the beads, use thick thread or several strands of fine thread. A needle will help you draw a knot up close to the bead.

Use a needle to knot right up to the edge of the bead.

Linking Beads

There are many other ways, besides using bead strands, to make bracelets. Link together groups of beads in similar colors with head or eye pins to hang as charms. You can wire each bead individually, which is quite time-consuming but produces an expensive-looking finish, or work the beads in small groups. To make the beads go further and use up leftover beads, insert short lengths of chain between each group of beads.

To make charms, use a head pin, a particularly useful finding for making charms because the flat head prevents beads from sliding off the pin. If the head pin slips through the bead hole, add a small stopper bead first. Slide the beads onto the pin in the order you want, trim the wire with wire cutters if necessary, and then turn a loop with round-nosed pliers. The loop can then be attached to a bead bracelet with a jump ring or opened slightly and joined directly to a chain bracelet.

Eye pins are ideal for linking beads together because they already have a preformed loop in one end. Use short pins for single beads and longer ones for groups of beads. Slide the beads onto each pin, trim the wire, and turn a loop, just as you would with a head pin. To link the beads together, use jump rings or open up a loop on the pin and join to the next loop. Make sure you close the loops securely or they will come undone when you wear them.

You can substitute jeweler's wire for the head and eye pins. To make charms, you will need to turn a small spiral in the end with round-nosed pliers. You can then leave this protruding as a decorative effect or turn it under so that the bottom bead sits on it. For linking beads, simply turn a loop in each end with pliers.

Multistrand Bracelets

To create more elaborate bracelets, work with multiple strands and add special clasps and other decorative findings. Multistrand bracelets can simply be several bead strands joined to one another or to an ornate spacer bar. More elaborate designs can be worked on more than one thread, split and worked individually, then brought back together.

To make the most basic multistrand bracelet, bead lots of strands of similar lengths. Finish the ends with calotte crimps and link the loops of these together in a jump ring. The ends can then be disguised with a pretty bell cap (see *Finishing Techniques*). To use end spacer bars, select one with the same number of holes as the number of threads you are using—usually two, three, or five—finish each beaded strand with a calotte crimp,

and join them directly or with jump rings to holes on the bar. You can also incorporate decorative spacer bars in the design, taking each thread through a hole as if it were a bead. Make sure you keep the threads in a straight line.

For a pretty variation on the multistrand design, work a bracelet on two or more threads, stringing beads onto all the threads for part of the design and individual threads at other points. As you get more experienced, try twisting or braiding the threads when they are worked on separately.

With more complicated bracelets such as these, it is important that you work out your design first and keep both sides of the bracelet symmetrical.

Finishing Techniques

How you finish a bracelet can make or break your design. To get a truly professional look, use findings—the tiny metal components used to link, join, and complete a design. Jump rings link together two or more pieces, such as a calotte crimp to a bracelet clasp, or groups of beads and charms to a bracelet, so they hang freely. To keep the shape of the ring, and to

Hold a jump ring with two pairs of pliers positioned at either side of the joint. Gently twist the ends away from each other sideways to open, and twist back again to close.

ensure that the two ends meet perfectly again, open the rings at the joint using pliers (two pairs of pliers are ideal), twisting the ends away from each other sideways rather than just pulling them apart. To close, simply twist the ends back again so that they meet exactly. Practice opening and closing them successfully.

End knots can look ugly and need to be disguised. For single-strand bracelets, a calotte crimp is usually sufficient; its preformed loop can be joined to a jump ring and a clasp.

Place the knot at the end of a length of thread in the cup of a calotte crimp and squeeze the two halves together using needle-nosed pliers.

There are several calotte crimp designs to choose from. Round calottes look like tiny metal beads when they are closed. They are hinged either at the side or bottom and have a gap for the thread to pass through. For sideways-opening calottes, position the knot in the "cup" of one half and use needle-nosed pliers to squeeze the two sides together. Make sure the thread is going in the right direction before you secure the crimp. If you are using calottes that open from the loop end, you will need to pass the thread through a small gap in the hinged end before knotting, then close in the same way as before. Use square calottes for

For this different style of calotte crimp, the thread is pushed through a hole in the base of the crimp before knotting. The two halves are then squeezed together.

These tiny crimp beads, used most often when working with tiger tail, are squeezed tightly with flat-nosed pliers to secure the loop in the tiger tail.

thick cord or thong; they are open on one side, which is where you insert the thread. With needle-nosed pliers, fold one side over the thread and then the other side to secure the thread. An alternative is crimp beads, tiny metal beads, that hold loops in the ends of nylon line or tiger tail. Simply thread them into position and squeeze firmly with pliers to secure.

Use calottes on multistrand bracelets when you are attaching a decorative end spacer, but if the design has lots of strands, add a bell cap to hide the calottes. This is a bell-shaped metal cap with a central hole. Slip the loops of the calottes onto a jump ring, but before closing the ring, push it through the loop of an eye pin.

A bell cap conceals a collection of knots or just adds a decorative end to a bracelet. Slip the open eye of an eye pin through a calotte loop in the tiger tail. Close it securely. Push the pin through the central hole in the cap, and trim and turn a loop in the opposite end.

Insert the pin through the hole in the cap, trim it to about ⅜ inch / 1 cm with wire cutters, and turn a loop with round-nosed pliers. Bell caps are often very ornate and come in a variety of sizes. Use the smaller ones as decorative ends on single-strand bracelets.

Once you have successfully concealed the knots, complete the bracelet with a clasp. Choose a style to suit your design: screw clasps and spring rings are the simplest and most discreet in appearance. Two-part clasps are often more decorative (they can be patterned or set with pearls or diamanté), and they can have more than one hole, which makes them ideal for multistrand bracelets. To attach a clasp to a bracelet, open up a jump ring and slip it through the loop on the calotte and the hole in the bracelet clasp, then close the ring. Two-part clasps have a corresponding catch, but for a spring-ring to the other end of the bracelet to complete the clasp.

A clasp adds the perfect finishing touch to a bracelet. To attach, simply insert an open jump ring through the loop at the end of the thread (or the loop of a calotte crimp) and through the loop on the clasp at the same time.

BEAD IDEAS

A VISIT TO YOUR LOCAL CRAFTS STORE WILL REVEAL AN array of beads to use in making your bracelet. Or be adventurous and use objects you can find at home, such as pasta shapes or feathers from a feather duster, to substitute for beads. If you choose to make your own beads, try unusual materials, such as newspaper and magazine cuttings, colored foil, or fabric scraps.

Clay Beads

One of the most effective materials to use is polymer clay. It is available in a fantastic range of colors, molds easily, and sets hard in a low-temperature oven. There are several comparable brands available, each with their own malleability, baking time, and color selection.

Plain beads in a single color can be molded into any shape you want and then decorated with acrylic paints (water-based paints don't cover as well). To make the beads, first knead the clay until it is soft and pliable, then roll it out into a log shape, ¼ to ¾ inch / .5 to 2 cm in diameter, depending on how big you want the bead to be. For tube beads, cut the log into equal lengths and pierce the center with a toothpick or knitting needle. Pierce the bead from both ends to get neat holes; if you just push the stick straight through, make sure that you smooth the rough edges where the stick emerges.

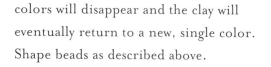

Round beads are made in the same way but each piece of clay is shaped into a ball in the palms of your hands. Pierce holes with a toothpick as above. Square beads are also made from a long log that is then flattened into a square against the edge of a knife or piece of wood. Cut to size and pierce as before. Add texture and detail to plain beads of any shape by pressing modeling tools, coins, and so on, against the surface, or by adding small strips or dots of other colors.

Experiment with several colors for more exciting finishes, such as marbling or millefiori. To create a marbled effect, roll out logs of two or more colors and wrap them around each other. Knead these together, roll them back into a larger log, folding it in half and twisting until the colors are blended. Be careful not to knead too much or the individual colors will disappear and the clay will eventually return to a new, single color. Shape beads as described above.

Millefiori or "thousand flower" beads are slightly more complicated, but rewarding to make once you have mastered the techniques. Begin with a core color—either a plain log or two colors rolled together. Then place other logs in different colors around the core, completely surrounding it. The colors are usually placed in a regular pattern and must be gently pressed together to ensure no air is trapped inside. The whole cane is then wrapped in another sheet of clay, carefully rolled out to a diameter of about ¼ inch / .5 cm, and cut into tiny slices that are pressed on an unbaked base bead to cover it.

Safety Note

Always read the instructions given on the polymer clay package. This clay gives off fumes, especially as it bakes, and should be used in a well-ventilated room.

Paper Beads

Using paper is one of the easiest and cheapest ways to make beads. The simplest papier-mâché beads can be made by shaping pieces of newspaper into a ball and then layering pasted strips of newspaper over it. For a smoother finish, layer the paper strips over a ball of plasticine. When the ball is completely dry, cut it in half with a craft knife and remove the plasticine to lighten the paper beads. Glue the two halves of the bead back together and conceal the joint with another layer of paper before decorating.

To make rolled paper beads, use old wrapping paper or magazines, or paint your own designs onto plain paper; then cut into strips or elongated triangles, and roll up tightly around a toothpick. To give the finished beads a sheen and a durable finish, paint them with clear nail polish.

Fabric Beads

You can use fabric to make all kinds of beads that can be decorated with embroidery or sewn stitches, or even with tiny beads. To make little puffs of fabric, cut the fabric out in circles, hem the edges, and draw up the edges. For tube beads, strips of fabric can be joined and gathered at either end. To give them shape, wrap them over a cardboard base or stuff with a little padding.

Wooden Beads & Pressed Cotton Beads

Most craft suppliers stock unvarnished wooden beads and pressed cotton balls in a variety of sizes. These are both easy to paint and decorate in your own individual style. Support the beads on wooden skewers, tops of pencils, or old paintbrush handles while painting, and leave to dry on a knitting needle stuck in a block of plasticine or polystyrene. Keep patterns simple. If you want to use several colors, let each color dry before starting the next. When you are finished, protect the surface with a coat of clear varnish or nail polish.

Miscellaneous Bead Ideas

Roll ordinary kitchen foil or colored candy foil wrappers to make bead shapes. Pierce the center with a sharp needle and thread into bracelets. Or add colored foil as a decorative final layer on a papier-mâché bead. Salt dough, which needs to bake in a low-temperature oven for several hours, is another good medium for making beads of different shapes. Both foil and clay can be painted and decorated to suit your design.

Pasta, seeds, nuts, and even washers can be painted, decorated, and strung into spectacular bracelets—no one will ever guess their origins. Use your imagination, and you will discover that all sorts of bits and pieces—safety pins, colorful paper clips, and even rubber bands can be turned into jewelry.

CREATING A DESIGN

Finding Inspiration

THE STARTING POINT IN ANY DESIGN IS FINDING INSPIRATION. Ideas for jewelry designs can come from a visit to a museum or a library. Look to the ancient Egyptian, Roman, and Celtic civilizations, as well as the more recent Arts and Crafts and Art Deco periods, for ideas. A walk in the country or along the seashore can put you in touch with one of the greatest and most economical design source libraries: Mother Nature. Flowers and foliage, rocks and minerals, insect and animal life all can spur the imagination. The sky provides us with the sun, moon, and star motifs that are perfect for interpreting into jewelry forms. The sea washes up shells on the beach and sculpts pebbles and wood into interesting shapes.

Don't forget the materials you have on hand. Beads and fabrics can fall accidentally and often haphazardly together to create striking and unusual combinations. Paints and decorative finishes are fun to experiment with. Clays can be molded into unusual shapes and given textured finishes.

Working Out a Design

Once you have found your inspiration, try to sketch out different ideas on paper. You will need a sketch book, tracing paper, pencils, colored crayons, felt tip markers (including gold and silver markers), an eraser, and a pencil sharpener. You don't have to draw works of art; rough sketches will suffice. Consider buying a special jewelry tray that has channels for the beads to easily plan and make bracelets in two or three different lengths.

For simple bead bracelets, start with a center point of interest, such as one of the beads you intend to use. Decide on the length you want (see *Stringing and Knotting* above). Then sketch the sides, keeping them symmetrical—though this is not as important as it is with necklaces, the bracelet will look odd if one side is obviously different from the other.

After working out your basic design, pick the thread, clasp, and end fittings. To calculate how many beads you will need, count the number of beads that fit into 1 inch / 2.5 cm, then multiply this by the length required. Write down the findings you will need next to your design sketch. If you want to try any unusual paint effects or create complex millefiori beads, experiment with paints on paper before moving on to a sample bead.

Basic BRACELETS

Basic bracelets can be as bold or as discreet as you like depending on the style of the design and the materials you choose to use. You can make sassy cuffs from brightly painted cork slices strung onto elastic; transform a simple circle of cardboard into a striking contemporary bangle using basic papier-mâché techniques; or create beautiful effects with ordinary safety pins and a few beads.

When designing basic bracelets, consider the overall size and balance of the design. If you use your hands a lot, a bracelet will be irritating if it is too big and gets in the way. You should be able to get the bracelet on and off your wrist easily, so choose a clasp that is easy to open with one hand or thread the beads or bead substitutes onto fine elastic. Shirring elastic is ideal but it is a good idea to work with a double thread on designs that use heavy beads. Try decorative fancy cord elastic available in fun, bright colors or metallic finishes to color-coordinate with the beads. Be careful to balance your design, making sure that any central detail is perfectly positioned and any repeated motifs (like a group of beads) are spaced at regular intervals along the bracelet.

Once you have mastered the step-by-step techniques, you can play with each basic bracelet design to make an attractive variation on a theme. Paint cork slices with decorative details or simply sand and varnish them to reveal their true natural beauty. Experiment with safety pins and beads in different sizes. Swap the hematite and pearl beads for a stunning collection of ornate buttons to make a glamorous bracelet for special occasions.

Jazz Age
CORK CUFF

Design Tips

Instead of painting the corks, sand them smooth with an emery board and use several coats of clear varnish to bring out the grain—thread them together with wooden beads to complete the natural look.

Pierce the corks from side to side instead of just through the middle for a different effect.

Experiment with cutting different shapes out of the cork—trim the curved sides for square slices.

Vary the width of the cork slices.

Make beads from Fimo or papier-mâché, choosing colors to coordinate or contrast with the painted cork.

Paint a design on the exposed edges of the cork, or add glittery jewels to add another dimension.

T HE INGENIOUS USE OF ORDINARY, EVERYDAY materials or recycled unwanted materials can produce striking and unusual jewelry designs—there is nothing more rewarding than creating something from nothing and it has the added advantage of costing very little, too. Discarded wine bottle corks were collected from friends and relatives to make this fun bangle. They are sterilized, cut into thick slices, and painted jazzy colors before being threaded on to elastic that makes it easy to get on and off the wrist. The slices can be sanded to produce a perfectly smooth finish or left with rough edges, creating a more textured look.

You Will Need

A selection of corks
Sterilizing tablet
Craft knife
Emery board
Knitting needle
Wooden skewers
Foam, polystyrene, or plasticine
(to hold skewers)
Gesso
Paintbrush
Artist's acrylic paints
Varnish
Shirring elastic
Sewing needle
Black plastic beads

Getting Started

Before you begin the project, sterilize the corks with sterilizing tablets following package instructions and let them dry. To help keep the rest of the beads from falling off while you thread the corks and beads, secure the free end of the thread to a larger bead.

JAZZ AGE CORK CUFF

Using a craft knife and working on a cutting mat or work bench, cut the corks into slices approximately ¼ inch / .6 cm wide.

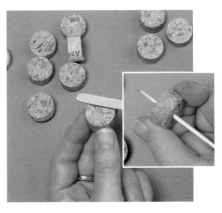

Use an emery board to smooth the edges of the cork, if required. Pierce a central hole in each slice with a knitting needle.

Thread the corks onto wooden skewers and paint all the slices with gesso. To hold the skewers upright while the corks dry, stick them into a piece of foam, plasticine, or polystyrene. When the gesso is dry, paint the slices in the colors of your choice. A final coat of varnish will give them a durable, longer-lasting finish.

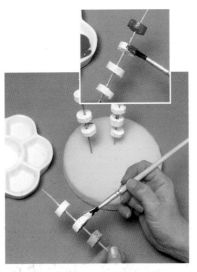

Thread the needle with a double length of elastic and secure the end to a bead. Thread on the corks and beads until the bracelet fits around your wrist when slightly stretched. Knot the end securely— a blob of super glue on the knot will give it added strength.

Variations on a Theme

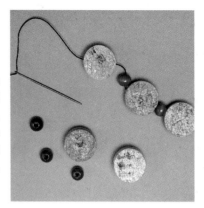

2. Thread a needle with elastic, fasten an end to a stopper bead, and thread the elastic through the corks and wooden beads.

1. For this variation, sand smooth cork slices that are narrower than the preceding project and pierce a hole from side to side using a large needle. Make sure the cork is free of dust, then paint with several coats of varnish, leaving each coat to dry before applying the next.

3. Add enough cork slices and beads to fit around your wrist when slightly stretched. Knot securely.

Painting a pattern on the edges of the cork slices gives the cuff a totally different look (right).

Beaded
BRAIDS

Design Tips

Watch for interesting antique braids at yard sales and consignment shops—they can be found as decoration on anything from cushions to hats.

◉

Choose colors that will coordinate with a favorite outfit for a special occasion.

◉

Experiment with different widths of braid to create different effects.

◉

Choosing the right size, style, or color of beads is essential to creating the right finished look—a hematite and pearl braid, for example, is perfect for a sophisticated bracelet to go with evening wear.

◉

The bead combination used for the braid project here would also look stylish on a black velvet bracelet. For a summer look, try adding a collection of mother-of-pearl buttons to a cream or white velvet band.

DECORATIVE BRAIDS ARE USUALLY USED TO TRIM fashion items or furnishings for the home, but here they have been completely transformed into unusual bracelets. Braid, ribbons, and even fancy cords can all be jazzed up and given a new purpose with simple bead embroidery. For a subtle, sophisticated look, choose a design that highlights the pattern or shape of the braid; or to create really impressive bracelets, completely cover the ribbon or braid with a collection of different ornate beads, buttons, or a combination of both.

You Will Need

A length of braid
Beads
Tailor's chalk
Sewing needle
Sewing thread or
invisible thread
Seed beads

Getting Started

Use invisible thread or sewing thread that matches the beads and braid you are working with. The seed beads should be in colors that coordinate with the other materials as well.

BEADED BRAIDS

1.

Cut a length of braid long enough to fit around your wrist, plus enough for turnings. Oversew or glue raw ends to neaten.

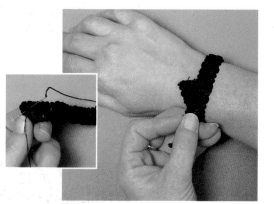

2.

Lay the braid out on a flat surface and work out your design. Use tailor's chalk to mark the required position for each bead.

4.

Join a double thread to the center of an end. String on 3 beads that match those used to work the design, then fasten off the thread close to the start position so that the beads form a "tab." At the opposite end, join a double thread to the center and thread on enough seed beads to make a loop that will slip neatly over the "tab" to join the two sides of the braid together.

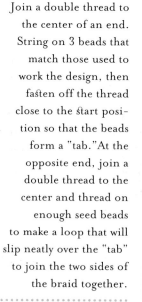
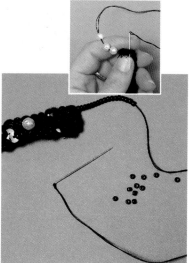

3.

Sew each bead in place individually, making sure it is secure.

Variations on a Theme

1. Using invisible thread, sew coordinating beads to a velvet scalloped braid, attaching them between scallops.

2. Add a scalloped edge in contrasting silvery beads by threading 7 beads onto the thread before taking it through one of the larger beads.

3. Take the thread through another silvery bead and back through the large bead used in step 1. Continue until the length of the braid has been worked on both sides.

4. Oversew a clasp to one end and a jump ring to the other. Put a blob of super glue on the joint of the jump ring to prevent the thread from slipping through.

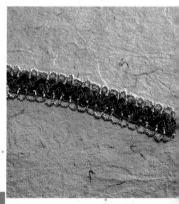

A simple piece of velvet ribbon can be transformed into a stunning bracelet with a collection of complementary buttons (all of which have shank backs) (right).

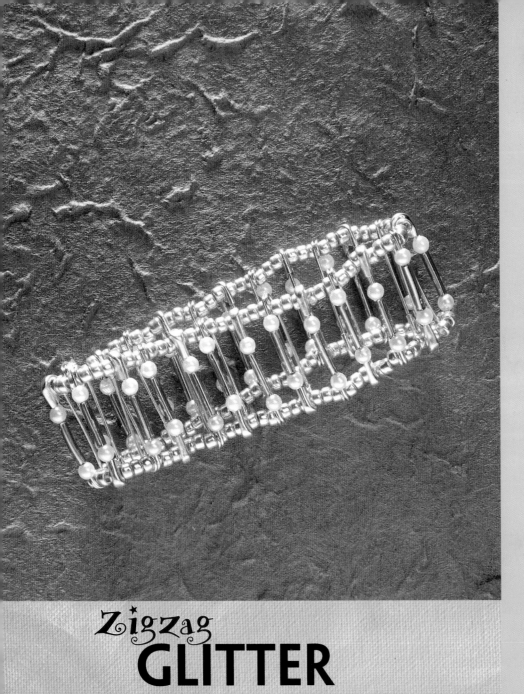

Zigzag GLITTER

Sketch your designs out first. Regular patterns make the most impressive results.

Smaller pins look best decorated with tiny rocailles or bugle beads.

Experiment with different-sized pins—larger ones can be transformed into quite bold designs and will take bigger beads.

To achieve the best shape, thread the pins onto the elastic alternately through the head and the tail.

Mixing gold- and silver-colored pins of the same size can create a stylish finish.

Use coordinating beads to separate the pins and make them go further if you only have a few.

Look for different colors of shirring elastic to coordinate with the bead design. Try gold or silver elastic to produce a more expensive-looking finished design.

T HE ORDINARY SAFETY PIN HAS BECOME THE
height of fashion more than once—it was an essential part
of punk rock fashion popular in the late 1970s and
then again more recently, when is was featured holding together
very expensive designer dresses. Decorated with bugle beads and
tiny pearls in pretty color
combinations, safety pins can be
threaded together in myriad
patterns to make unique pieces
of jewelry.

You Will Need

Small safety pins
Bugle beads and small pearls
Pliers
Sewing needle
Shirring elastic
2 large beads
Gold rocailles
Glue

Getting Started

Select about 22 safety pins and enough gold rocailles to thread
between the pins for this glittering bracelet. Be careful not to distort
the shape of the pin when using the pliers to join the two sides of
the heads.

ZIGZAG GLITTER

1.

Thread the beads onto each safety pin in the order required by your design.

2.

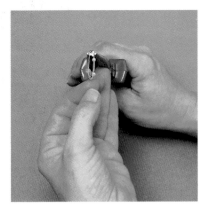

The head of each pin is closed so the elastic will not slip out. Using a pair of pliers, gently bring both sides of the head together.

3.

Using the pliers again, carefully squeeze together the edges of the head that hold the actual "pin."

4.

Thread the needle with shirring elastic and secure a large bead to prevent the design from falling off as you work. Take the needle through the tail of a pin, then through the spacer beads and head of the next pin. Alternate the pins and add the same amount of beads between them until they fit around your wrist when the elastic is slightly stretched.

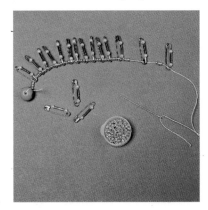

5.

Knot the elastic securely and add a blob of glue to strengthen it. To achieve a neater finish, push the knot inside a spacer bead to conceal it.

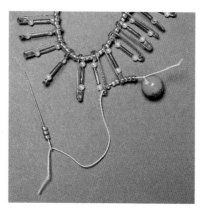

6.

Thread the elastic through the needle and tie it to a large bead again. Take the needle through the other end of the pins, adding the same number of beads between pins. Knot and finish in the same way as in step 5.

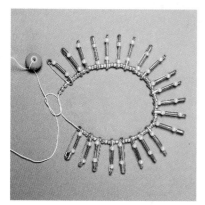

Variations on a Theme

Large silver pins look great threaded with long silver bugle beads and faux pearls. To create the stripe effect the pins with bugles have been threaded onto the elastic in pairs, with heads and tails facing and the pearl pins flipped in the opposite direction (right).

Plastic beads that look like amber have been used to make this cuff (far right).

Brilliant Sunburst
BANGLE

P APIER-MÂCHÉ AS A CRAFT IS ENJOYING A GREAT revival. It is versatile, costs very little, and needs only a small space to work in, which makes it a great medium for jewelry-making projects. Papier-mâché, which means "mashed paper" in French, has been used over the centuries to make a variety of objects, from side tables to jewelry boxes.

The technique shown in this project is one of the easiest: layers of pasted strips of torn paper are placed over a base shape or mold. Just be careful when building up the layers to ensure that they are smooth, with no air or lumps of paste trapped underneath. The contemporary shape of this bangle lends itself to bold, colorful designs but could look just as stylish decorated with small jewel stones or in less vibrant shades.

You Will Need

Firm cardboard
Pencil
Compass
Scissors
Wallpaper paste
Paste brush
Small strips of torn newspaper
PVA glue
Emery board
Gesso
Paintbrush
Tracing paper
Artist's acrylic paints
Fine paintbrush
Gold metallic marker pen
Varnish

Getting Started

Mix only a small amount of wallpaper paste for these papier-mâché bangles. Tear newspaper into small strips and put six to eight layers on each bangle, enough to create a firm, finished piece.

BRILLIANT SUNBURST BANGLE

1. Use the compass to draw 2 circles on the cardboard as shown: the inner circle with a radius of approximately 1½ inches / 4 cm and the outer circle with a radius of 2 ⅜ inches / 7 cm.

2. Cut out the shape using sharp scissors. Cutting lines radiating out from the center point makes it easier to get a more perfect inner circle.

3. Paste each newspaper strip and layer over the cardboard shape, covering both sides, including the outer and inner edges. Paint the last few with PVA glue instead of paste for a durable finish.

4. Use an emery board to lightly smooth any rough edges. Don't be too vigorous or this will spoil the surface. Brush off any dusty residue. Paint the bangle with artist's gesso. This acts as an undercoat and prevents the newsprint from showing through the painted finish.

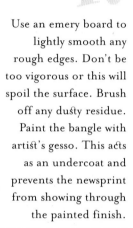

5.

Lay your tracing paper design on the surface of the bangle and lightly transfer it to both sides making sure the points meet at the outer and inner edges. Don't make the pencil lines too heavy or they won't be covered by the paint.

6.

Use a fine paintbrush to apply the colors of your choice, making sure both sides match at the inner and outer edges. Let each color dry before applying the next.

7.

To complete the project, outline the design carefully with a gold metallic marker pen and let it dry. Apply 2 to 3 coats of varnish following instructions for drying times.

Variations on a Theme

What a difference a change of colors makes (right).

The inspiration for this design comes from pretty blue and white china. The simple flowers have been painted freehand to give it a softer look. Practice the shapes on a piece of paper before working on the finished bangle (far right).

Fabric &
COPPER CUFF

Design Tips

Experiment with different types of fabric. Paint the PVA on a test piece of fabric first to check how many coats will be needed to get the rigidity you require.

Ⓢ

PVA gives some fabrics an obvious shine. Do a test piece and check that you are happy with the finish.

Ⓢ

You can achieve different effects by painting or embroidering the fabric first. Make sure you do a small test piece and paint with PVA as some embroidery threads can run colors.

Ⓢ

Cut motifs in different shapes, such as hearts or daisies, to cover the fabric joint.

Ⓢ

To make textured fabrics, such as linen, look expensively gilded, lightly brush them with metallic paint.

THE USE OF FABRIC IN JEWELRY DESIGN IS BECOMING more and more popular. This "soft" jewelry offers endless opportunities for innovative ideas. Even traditional crafts such as embroidery, quilting, and patchwork can all be applied to different jewelry designs. Stiffening fabric with PVA glue gives it another dimension, as this bangle bracelet illustrates. It is made from a strip of inexpensive linen scrim that has been painted with PVA glue. The PVA gives the fabric a clear plastic coating, almost invisible to the eye, that helps keep it rigid and in shape. For a decorative finishing touch, spirals and a plain medallion motif have been glued to a diamond of fabric. These were made from a garden plant label, but you can also buy sheet copper from craft and sculpting suppliers. This kind of jewelry is pure fun but obviously is not as durable as anything made out of metal or plastic.

Getting Started

To determine the right size of fabric to use for this bracelet, cut a strip of fabric 2" / 5 cm wide. Fold to form a circle that will fit easily over your hand. Add a little extra fabric for the overlap. Make sure you use clear-drying glue that is suitable for metal surfaces.

FABRIC & COPPER CUFF

Neaten any raw edges of the cloth by gluing them to the side of the cloth that will not be seen. Cut out 2, 2 inch / 5 cm squares for the central motif and glue them together.

Make a tuck in each short end of fabric and secure it with a few oversew stitches.

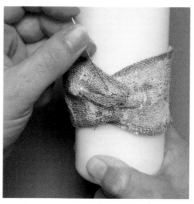

Pour the PVA into a dish and, resting the fabric on a ceramic surface, paint the side that will not show with PVA, making sure the glue goes into the folds formed by the tucks. Paint the center motif and leave it on a ceramic surface.

Wrap the fabric bangle around a round plastic squeeze bottle or ceramic dish that has been rubbed with soft soap or Vaseline so that the fabric can be easily removed when dry. Pin it in place and let it dry.

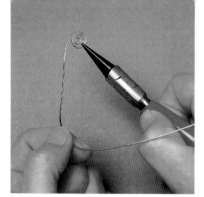

5. Cut the tie of the copper plant label in half. Turn each half around the tips of round-nosed pliers to make decorative spirals.

6. Cut a 1 inch / 2.5 cm square of copper from the plant label, and using a suitable adhesive, glue it to the center of a side of the motif.

7. Turn the fabric motif on its side to make a diamond and glue the spirals to the wrong side as shown. Let dry. Glue the motif to the stiffened bangle, covering the joint.

Variations on a Theme

Using red and white gingham this time, the center is a neatened strip of fabric that has been stiffened and wrapped around tightly (right).

Narrow strips of candy-striped cotton have been painted with PVA and wrapped around an ordinary plastic bangle, giving it a brand new look (far right).

Charm
BRACELETS

You can make all kinds of charm bracelets, whether you use fun, simple beads, daring sequins, or even ordinary metal washers. Shells collected from the seashore can be drilled and wired to make charms that look wonderful falling from a raffia braid. Or mold, roll, and sculpt modeling clay into an eclectic mix of inspired shapes, from playing-card motifs to millefiori slices.

When hanging charms around a bracelet, it is especially important to work out your design. Consider the weight of the charms before choosing a basic bracelet of beads or a length of chain. Space charms evenly along the length of the bracelet for the best effect. It is also important to select a clasp that is easy to open with one hand so that getting the bracelet on and off is effortless. The balance of the design is also crucial; hang large charms from a medium or heavy chain, not a fine chain. In most cases it is better if the design is worked symmetrically, but when using a great number of the same beads, a mistake will hardly be noticeable.

The bracelets that follow are designed to fire your imagination and spur you on to create your own variations once you have mastered the techniques shown in the step-by-step projects. Design different styles of millefiori canes to slice and turn into colorful charms. Experiment with other ways of linking metal washers, and vary the color combinations and sizes of the bead charms to alter the look of the *Toolbox Pearls* bracelet. Bring in other elements of the sea to give the shell charm bracelet a truly natural look. Or research the myriad colors of mosaic tiles to get inspiration for your own variation on the tile charm bracelet.

Toolbox
PEARLS

Design Tips

For a bold design, hang charms from each of the jump rings used to link the chain together. For a more delicate look, space them out at regular intervals.

◎

Experiment with washers and beads in different sizes.

◎

Washers usually come in chrome or brass finishes but can also be painted with hobby enamels and even car paints. For a completely different look, choose vibrant shades and hang brilliantly colored glass beads as charms.

◎

Lightly sand rusty washers and give them a new lease on life with a coat of enamel paint.

◎

Other toolbox finds like hexagonal nuts, butterfly nuts, bolts, and split rings can all be wired into charms.

◎

Experiment with other unusual "charms"—parts from a broken watch, old buttons with shank fastenings, and even miniatures from a doll house can all be used to create unusual bracelets.

TURNING JUNK INTO STYLISH JEWELRY CAN BECOME an addictive hobby. Once hooked, you'll find yourself looking at all kinds of mundane objects in a new light. A basic household toolbox, for example, is an absolute treasure trove for an innovative designer, full of unusual bits and pieces that can be transformed into unique pieces of jewelry. All it takes is a little creative thought.

This project for a stylish charm bracelet proves the point—ordinary metal washers have been cleverly linked together to make an unusual chain from which to hang bead charms collected from broken pieces of jewelry. Flea markets and rummage sales are great hunting grounds for unusual objects.

Washers
Jump rings
Pliers
Head pins
Beads
Wire cutters
Bracelet clasp

Getting Started

Make sure that as you handle the washers and jump rings, the pliers do not scrape or scratch their surface. With a piece of string, measure your wrist for a bracelet that will fit loosely without falling off.

TOOLBOX PEARLS

Use pliers to open up
a jump ring and slip it
through a washer. Close
securely. Open the
next jump ring, slip it
through the first washer,
and add another before
closing. Continue in
the same way until they
form a chain.

Insert a head
pin through each
bead and trim away any
excess wire, leaving
enough to turn into a
loop using pliers.

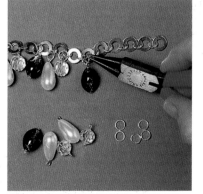

Slip jump rings through
the top loop of each
bead, and join these to
a jump ring on the
chain, making sure it is
closed securely.

Join a jump ring to the
last washer in the chain,
slipping through the
loop on a bolt clasp at
the same time. (This
will open and close over
the jump ring at the
beginning of the chain.)

Variations on a Theme

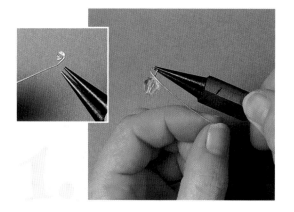

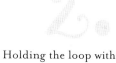

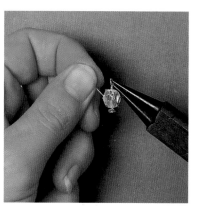

Holding the loop with pliers, wrap the wire back down the bead toward the base. You can do this as many times as you want, depending on the look you prefer and the size of the bead.

Wrap beads with soft jeweler's wire for a fashionable variation. Using the tips of a pair of pliers, turn a tiny spiral at the end of a length of wire. Bend the wire at a 45°-angle to the spiral and insert it through the central hole of a bead so that the bead "sits" on the spiral. Turn the wire over the pliers to make a small loop at the top of the bead, then wrap it around itself tightly, once or twice, to secure.

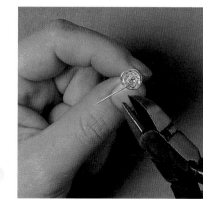

To finish, wrap the wire around itself, between the bead and the spiral, and trim with wire cutters.

Join the beads to the bracelet with jump rings.

Bits and pieces from a household toolbox have been used as charms for this variation (right).

Sparkling
SEQUINS

Design Tips

Experiment with different
charm designs, suspending them
in a variety of ways.

⟳

Attach a mixture of solid and
open-centered oval sequins in a
mix of colors.

⟳

Craft and bead specialists often sell
sequin sweepings that contain quite
unusual shapes. These cost less than
normal as they are literally swept up
from where they fall during packing.
They are cleaned and then bagged as
an assortment.

⟳

Use a fine needle to pierce a hole first,
then enlarge it carefully if necessary
with a thicker needle or by running
the finer one around and around
the hole—a large needle will
shred some smaller sequins. A piece
of cork under the sequin will make
this process easier.

⟳

Create pretty theme bracelets by
stringing together associated sequin
shapes, such as stars and moons, or
birds, flowers, and butterflies.

SEQUINS DO NOT NORMALLY SPRING TO MIND WHEN considering materials for making bracelets, but they can be made into quite spectacular and unusual designs. They are available in a variety of shapes, a kaleidoscopic range of colors, and are inexpensive, all of which makes them perfect for fun jewelry designs. Sequin motifs in the shape of flowers, leaves, birds, and butterflies make fun charms suspended from a sequin or bead bracelet, while the classic smooth-surface discs look stylish, especially if they have a hologram finish. You can mix them together in wild color combinations or two-tone shades. Sequins that come with holes to one side are the easiest to use and can be made into instant charms, but other designs can be used too. They are all easy to pierce with the point of a needle.

You Will Need

Flower-shaped sequins
Rocaille beads
Clear-drying craft glue
Toothpick
Needle
Jump rings
Eye pins
Round-nosed pliers
Wire cutters
Nylon thread or tiger tail
2 calotte crimps
Gold rocaille beads
Clasp

Getting Started

You will need lots of tiny rocaille beads that color-coordinate with the flower-shaped sequins, as well as gold rocaille beads. The number of sequin charms that you use will vary depending on how close together you attach them.

SPARKLING SEQUINS

1.

Glue rocaille beads in shades of the same color over the center hole of each flower sequin that will be used as a charm. The number of charms needed will vary depending on how close together you attach them.

2.

Use the point of a needle to make a small hole in a petal of each flower sequin to attach a jump ring. Twist the jump rings to open and insert them through the hole on each sequin that will be made into a charm.

3.

Thread 3 or 4 gold rocailles onto an eye pin. Trim the pin with wire cutters so that approximately ⅜ inch / 1 cm extends beyond the beads. Turn this into a loop using the tips of pliers.

4.

Measure and cut your chosen thread to fit around your wrist with room for knots, then knot the end and secure it to a calotte crimp. Thread on the sequins, taking the thread through the center hole with gold beads spaced between each sequin, adding charms as you work.

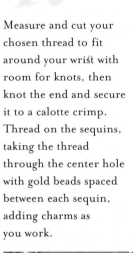

Variations on a Theme

5.
When the bracelet reaches the right length, finish it off with another knot secured in a calotte crimp. Twist open 2 jump rings and attach them to each calotte crimp. Complete the bracelet by attaching a clasp to a jump ring.

2.
Insert an open jump ring through each hole and then through the link on the chain at the same time. Close the jump ring securely.

1.
Hologram disc sequins can be made into fun bracelets. Cut a length of chain to fit your wrist and count the number of links on the chain. Choose a corresponding number of sequins, and use a needle to pierce a hole close to an edge of each sequin.

3.
The result is a melange of vividly colored hologram sequins, suspended from a length of chain.

Use just a few colors and fix interesting sequin shapes to make a more discreet elasticized bracelet (right).

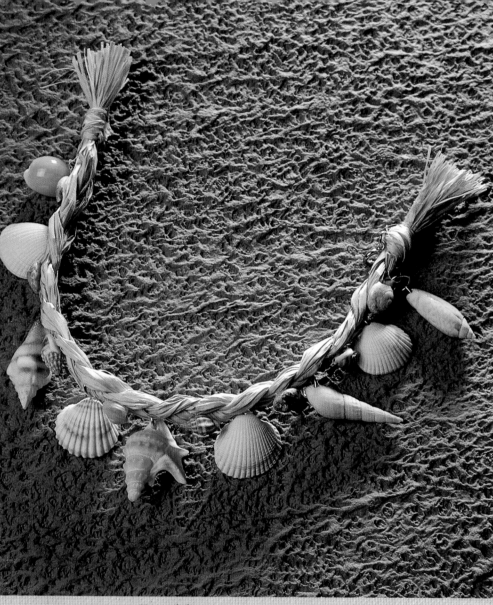

Seashell
CHARMS

Always treat shells with care; some of the prettiest can be very fragile. Painting them with a few coats of varnish or PVA glue will help make finer shells more sturdy as well as give them a shine.

Varnish gives subtle marking more definition.

Secure the shell on a piece of Blu Tak or plasticine when making holes. This helps prevents them from spinning under the drill.

Experiment with different materials to make the basic band—string, garden twine, or fine leather thongs work well. To make the band more distinctive, use macrame and knotting techniques.

Combine the shells with complementary beads that will show them off to their best advantage and not overpower them.

Experiment by incorporating other elements from the seashore, such as small pieces of interesting driftwood, starfish, and pretty pebbles.

SHELL JEWELRY IS AN IDEAL WAY TO SHOW OFF THE beautiful shapes, colors, and markings of seashells. Some shells are soft enough to take holes made with a needle or bradawl, but for others you will need a hand drill and a fine bit to make the holes. For a delightful charm bracelet similar to this project you need smallish shells for the charms and tiny shells to decorate the braid. Larger shells are best kept for making into pendants, threaded onto a thong, cord, or raffia. To make shell charms, you need to drill holes in a selection of shells and slip a jump ring through each. The rings are then closed securely through a raffia braid.

Getting Started

Select two sizes of shells for this seashell charm bracelet—tiny shells to decorate the band and nine or ten slightly larger shells to hang as charms. Use six strands of raffia about five times the length required for braiding and finishing. You can obtain raffia from craft suppliers and garden centers.

You Will Need

Small shells
Natural raffia
Large blunt-ended tapestry needle
Hand drill
$^1/_{16}$" / 1.5 mm drill bit
Plasticine or Blu Tak
Jump rings
Tweezers or pliers
All-purpose, clear-drying craft glue
Bolt ring clasp

SEASHELL CHARMS

1.

Knot 6 strands of raffia securely together at one end, divide them into 3 pairs, and braid together. The braid should be approximately 6 inches / 15 cm longer than you need.

2.

Cut an 8 inch / 20 cm length of raffia from the remaining strand and knot it over the braid approximately 3 inches / 8 cm down from the starter knot, leaving a 3 inch / 8 cm tail extending to the center of the bracelet.

Bind the rest neatly and tightly over the strand knot, covering it and leaving enough tail to thread back through the binding away from the bracelet. Thread the start tail through and cut off the knot at the beginning of the braid.

3.

Wrap the braid around your wrist and mark the required finished length, then bind as before. Trim the ends

to about ¾ inch / 1.9 cm from the binding and fray out to form a tassel.

4.

Drill a hole in each of the shells to be used as charms. Use a sharp drill bit and don't apply too much pressure or both the shell and the bit may shatter.

5.

Twist open the jump rings and insert them at regular intervals through the edge of the braid.

6.

Add the shells, positioning them on the ring so they all face in the same direction. Close the rings carefully and securely with pliers.

7.

Lay the band out flat and glue tiny shells directly onto the raffia. Use pliers to open up 2 jump rings and push them through the binding at each end. Slip the clasp onto a ring, then close both securely with pliers.

Variations on a Theme

Ordinary garden twine has been twisted and wrapped around itself to make a cord, then decorated with gold-brushed shells and shell-shaped metal beads (right).

Add shell charms to a pearl string for a completely different effect (far right).

Shimmering
MOSAICS

Design Tips

Lay the tiles out in front of you and work out a color scheme, then select complementary beads to use as charms.

Experiment with different ways of linking the tiles together. Spirals worked from silver wire can be turned into figure-eight links, spring-like coils, and ornate spirals.

Try gluing material like crushed egg shells to papier-mâché tile shapes to give them texture as well as color.

You can get bags of irregularly shaped tiles in fabulous colors. These can be embedded in Polyfilla, plaster, or air-dry clay shapes to create the interesting patterns more frequently associated with the craft of mosaics. If they are loose after the base has dried, glue them in place.

THESE MOSAIC TILES WERE DISCOVERED ON A STAND at a craft fair where the techniques for using them to create beautiful plaques and tabletops were being demonstrated. They illustrate perfectly how the most unusual materials can be transformed into stunning pieces of jewelry. The tiles are made from glass, which is not easy to drill, so large, thick jump rings are glued in place with epoxy adhesive so they can be linked together. The tiles can be obtained from craft specialists or tile suppliers. They come in a range of colors, from the pastels shown here to vivid pop art colors like orange, red, lime, green, and yellow.

You Will Need

6 small glass mosaic tiles
5 coordinating glass drop beads
12 large jump rings
Epoxy glue
7 small jump rings
5 triangle bails
Pliers
Two-part snap clasp

Getting Started

To keep the jump rings perfectly level as they dry, support them on another tile or lump of plasticine. Make sure that as you link the jump rings to the rings glued to the tiles, all the tiles are facing in the same direction.

SHIMMERINGS MOSAICS

1.

Squeeze a small amount of the epoxy onto a piece of thick cardboard, carefully cleaning the tips of the tubes. Mix the glue together thoroughly. Be careful not to get any on yourself.

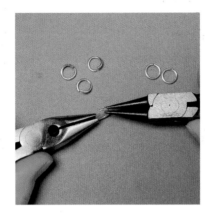

2.

Close the large jump rings so they lie flat.

3.

Following the guidelines given for the glue, stick a jump ring to the opposite corners on each tile. Make sure the ring extends beyond the tile so that you will be able to link tiles together later, when all rings are glued on.

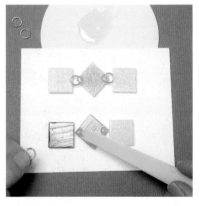

4.

After the large jump rings have dried on each tile, twist open the smaller jump rings and slip them through a large jump ring on each of the tiles, making sure the tiles have their right sides facing the same direction.

Close the jump rings so they join exactly.

Slip a triangle bail over the small linking jump ring and push one of its ends into a side of the hole at the top of a drop bead. Line up the other end of the bail with the opposite hole in the bead and squeeze the ends together to secure the bead.

Twist open a small jump ring and slip it through the last large jump ring at an end of the bracelet and a part of the clasp. Twist it back to secure. Repeat for the other part of the clasp to complete the bracelet.

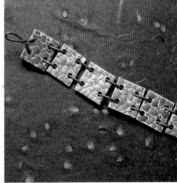

Variations on a Theme

The tiles themselves form the charms on this variation, with the jump rings glued to just a corner. A copper chain from an old necklace was used for the bracelet (right).

For a completely different mosaic look, crushed eggshell has been applied to a simple tile-shaped, papier-mâché base (far right).

Pack of Cards
BRACELET

Design Tips

To get the best finish from a polymer modeling clay, knead it well to soften it and remove any air bubbles.

Leave the clay wrapped in a plastic bag on top of a towel on a warm radiator or oven to help speed up the softening time.

Glue jewel stones to the clay shapes to add sparkle to the charms.

A trip to a professional kitchen shop can provide a wealth of inspiration and a variety of cookie cutters or molds in different shapes.

Different shapes can be cut from cardboard templates if cookie cutters aren't available. Then cut the outline in the clay with a craft knife.

BASIC COOKIE CUTTERS PROVIDE THE INSPIRATION for this fun charm bracelet. Tiny flat-backed jewel stones add the glittering finishing touch. The charms are made from polymer modeling clay. Once the clay has been kneaded and warmed in your hands, it can be rolled out just like pastry, which makes it ideal for using with cutters. The shapes that inspired this project are slightly smaller than most cookie cutters and are therefore the perfect size for charms. The modeling clays come in a wide range of colors that can be used simply as they are, blended together to create marbled effects, or painted and textured to produce totally unique finishes.

Getting Started

Before you begin, cut five or six lengths of black cotton thread to the length of the circumference of your wrist plus an extra six inches for knotting. Make sure you use either clear-drying craft glue or glue specially formulated for synthetic clays. Always be careful to keep each polymer clay color separate through the steps of this project.

You Will Need

Blocks of red and black polymer clay
Rolling pin
Shaped cutters or cardboard to draw and cut out templates
Toothpick
Varnish
Paintbrush
Tiny flat-backed jewel stones
Tweezers
All purpose, clear-drying craft glue
Black thread
2 square calottes
Needle
Black beads
Jump rings for each charm and both ends of bracelet
Round- and needle-nosed pliers
Clasp

PACK OF CARDS BRACELET

Knead the clay thoroughly to soften it and make it malleable. Work it between your thumbs and fingers and roll it between the palms of your hands. Roll each color out separately to a depth of approximately ¼ inch / .6 cm. Be careful to keep the colors separate.

Press the cutters onto the clay using even pressure. Carefully smooth any indentations with the tips of your fingers.

Use an emery board to smooth any rough edges, then paint each shape with a coat of varnish. Let dry.

Pierce a hole in the top of each charm, using a toothpick or needle. Bake the charms in a low-temperature oven following the guidelines given on the packet.

5. Add a small blob of all-purpose glue to the back of each jewel stone and position on the charms.

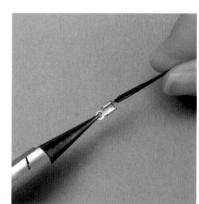

6. Working with all the strands of thread together, make a large knot at the end of the group of threads and position it inside a square calotte. Squeeze both sides of the calotte over the threads to secure. Thread on the beads to make a strand of the required length.

7. Twist open a jump ring and slip it through the hole at the top of each charm. Place the charms at regular intervals between the beads and close the jump rings securely. Complete the bracelet by attaching a clasp and jump ring to each end of the bracelet.

Variations on a Theme

Blue gemstones add the finishing touch to bright yellow flower charms cut out of synthetic clay (right).

Gold paint and crystal jewel stones give these teardrop charms a glamorous finishing touch (far right).

1000 Flowers
CHARMS

Design Tips

A book on the history of beads or old pieces of jewelry can provide inspiration for different millefiori designs.

⊙

Sketch designs on paper and color with felt tip pens or paints that match the shades of the clays.

⊙

Use colors in brilliant contrasting combinations or simple pairs such as black and white.

⊙

Cut out wedges of clay and substitute for or alternate with logs to get another style of design.

⊙

Experiment with more graphic designs like stripes and squares to make a change from the traditional flower.

⊙

Use scraps of clay leftover from other projects to make multicolored canes.

THE CHARMS FOR THIS UNUSUAL BRACELET ARE made from colorful synthetic clays, using a technique called *millefiori* which was developed by Venetian glass makers. The name means "a thousand flowers" because the Venetians could cut so many slices of the same flower pattern from one glass cane. The original glass beads were so highly prized all over the world that they were used as a form of currency to buy from the merchants who visited the busy port of Venice. The same basic techniques can be applied to polymer clays. The cane is built up around a core color that is surrounded by layers of different colors and finally wrapped in a sheet of clay. The completed cane is sliced to make the charms.

You Will Need

Blocks of Fimo in black, yellow, white, pink, and purple
Rolling pin
Craft knife
Toothpick
Varnish
15 to 20 triangle bails or large jump rings (1 for each charm)
Pliers
A length of chain (approximately 6"/ 15.2 cm)
Clasp

Getting Started

Knead the Fimo with your thumbs and fingers until really soft and pliable. This will make it much easier to roll and prevent cracks. Wash your hands when changing colors to prevent one from rubbing off on the other and spoiling the finished effect.

1,000 FLOWERS CHARMS

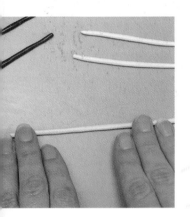

For the core of the cane, roll out a log of yellow clay with a diameter of approximately ¼ inch / .6 cm. Roll out 4 logs in purple and 4 in white clay to a similar length and diameter.

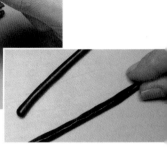

Place the purple and white logs alternately around the yellow log, as shown. Gently compress them together and roll the resulting cane between the palms of your hands to press out any air bubbles. Make another cane in exactly the same way, and 2 more where you substitute pink for the purple, so you will have 4 canes in all. Roll out 5 logs in black, making them slightly larger in diameter than the previous logs. Lay 4 of these out on a flat surface and pinch them along one side to make them wedge-shaped. These will be used in the next step to fill in the gaps between the other logs to make the whole cane round.

Using the unpinched black log as the core, place the 4 canes you made in step 2 alternately around it, with black wedges filling the gaps in between the logs. Gently compress all the colors together so there are no air pockets.

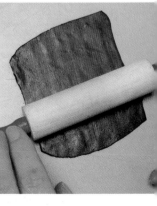

Roll out a sheet from the black clay with a depth of approximately ⅛ inch / .3 cm.

Wrap the sheet around the cane, smoothing the seam gently with your finger. Compress it together and roll it gently between your hands so there are no air pockets. You may find it easier to cut the cane into shorter lengths before wrapping with the last sheet of Fimo.

With a craft knife, cut the cane into ¼ inch / .6 cm slices and reshape them with your hands. Pierce a hole in each slice close to the edge and bake them in a low-temperature oven following instructions on the Fimo package. A finishing coat of varnish will bring out all the colors; leave to dry for 24 hours before joining the slices to the chain.

Completing the Bracelet

Count the number of links in the chain and decide whether to place the charms in every one or every other one. To join them to the chain, slip a triangle bail through a link in the chain and push one of its ends into one side of the hole at the top of a charm. Line up the other end of the bail with the opposite hole in the charm and squeeze the two ends together to secure the charm. Finish by attaching a clasp to one end of the chain and a jump ring to the other.

Variations on a Theme

To make these square charms (right), the clay is cut into small slabs that are then laid on top of one another to form the pattern.

Leftover clays from other projects have been used to make this striking design. The basic cane is the same for each charm but it was cut into smaller lengths and each wrapped with a different color (far right).

Multistrand & Linked
BRACELETS

Multistrand and linked bracelets open up the possibility for more creative designs, using lots of different elements. You can create glamorous bracelets using faux pearls and diamanté and finish them with authentic style clasps; make beautiful, colorful beads that mimic real marble from pressed cotton balls and old nail polish; or create striking contemporary designs from simple cardboard.

As with all bracelets, consider the weight and overall balance of the bracelet when you design multistrand and linked bracelets. Use tiger tail and nylon line for simple strings of beads because they are strong and hard to break. Be careful to balance your design, making sure any central detail is positioned at the actual center of the bracelet. Check that repeated motifs and patterns use the same colors and are worked to the same size and tension. It is important that a bracelet is the right length; if it is too loose, it will continually catch on things and probably break; if it is too tight, it will affect your circulation and irritate your skin. To add a special finishing touch, include ornate clasps with several holes to join multiple threads. You can buy these from craft suppliers or hunt for authentic originals at antique fairs and rummage sales.

Once you have mastered the techniques in the step-by-step projects, you'll be ready to try the variations on each of the following designs. Use paper string instead of embroidery threads for an unusual linked bracelet. Experiment with different color combinations and sizes of beads to make new variations of the *Daisy Chain* design. Or use different paint techniques to give pressed cotton balls a special finish that imitates precious stones and minerals.

Sparkling
PEARLS

Design Tips

Use genuine antique beads to give a really special finish, especially if the design is inspired by the past.

◎

Vary the size and finish of the pearl beads to create more interesting effects—baroque pearls and freshwater pearls, for example, have different textures that are a change from the classic smooth bead.

◎

Experiment with different color combinations—jet black would look stunning with the faux diamond stones. For a completely different look, combine pastel-colored synthetic pearls with toning jewel stones.

◎

Swap the jewel stones for ornately decorated or diamanté-encrusted spacer bars.

◎

Choose colors to suit a favorite outfit or occasion; substitute other beads for the crystals to create a look that is more suitable for day wear.

THE DECADE OF THE 1930s WAS A GREAT ONE FOR creative jewelry design. Style books on this period or old fashion magazines are excellent sources of inspiration for your own individual creations. The 1930s-inspired bracelet in this project is simple yet stylish and worked in a combination of pearl beads and crystal stones. The sparkle from the diamond-like jewel stones makes this particular bead combination ideal for evenings, but the look of the bracelet can be totally transformed by choosing different colors, styles, and even sizes of beads. Pretty bracelets like these deserve to be finished off with attractive catches rather than plain bolt rings, but they shouldn't overpower the simplicity of the finished design. You can buy a variety of different styles from jewelry suppliers, but to discover more unusual and ornate designs, hunt for broken pieces of jewelry at an antiques fair or rummage sale.

You Will Need

Small pearl beads
3 glass-faceted jewelry stones and
sewing mounts (with 4 holes)
Flat or needle-nosed pliers
Tiger tail, nylon, or
strong cotton thread
2 calotte crimps
2 jump rings
Two-part clasp

Getting Started

Collect about 48 small pearl beads—the amount will vary, depending on the size of the beads and the finished length required. When working with jewelry stones, be careful not to scratch the stones with the pliers.

SPARKLING PEARLS

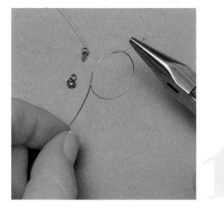

Cut 2 lengths of thread, each 6 inches / 15 cm longer than the required finished length. Make a knot in an end of each and neaten it with a calotte crimp.

Position the jewelry stones in their mounts, taking care to set them so they sit evenly. Squeeze the securing prongs down over the stone gently with flat or needle-nosed pliers, taking care not to damage the stone.

Start to string the beads onto the first thread, with 6 pearls followed by a jewel stone. Take the thread through 2 corresponding holes in the jewel stone.

Complete the first side, keeping the pattern regular and making sure all the jewel stones face the same way.

Double-check the length and make any adjustments to the pattern.

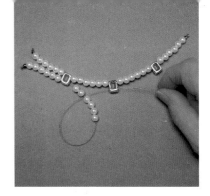

Work the second strand of the bracelet in the same way, taking it through the remaining 2 holes in the jewel stone.

Twist open a jump ring and slip it through both loops on the calottes at an end of the bracelet and a loop on the clasp.

Close it securely by twisting the ends back together with pliers. Repeat at the opposite end to complete the bracelet.

Variations on a Theme

This 3-strand variation uses diamanté-encrusted spacer bars and a dramatic clasp to add detail to an otherwise simple design (right).

Experimenting with different-sized beads creates a more dramatic look (far right).

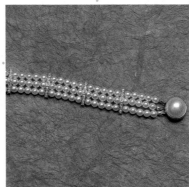

Harlequin
THREADS

Design Tips

Keep all embroidery thread to a reasonable length—anything 3 inches / 8 cm or more can be used—and sort them into color groups.

◎

Look up different ideas on knotting, weaving, and braiding threads.

◎

Experiment with jeweler's wire and pliers, and try making your own crimps if you can't find anything suitable for the materials you want to use.

◎

You can cover piping cord with scraps of fabric for another look, or even paint fabric with your own design.

◎

To give the threads a fine texture, string tiny beads onto embroidery thread and knot the thread on both sides of the bead to hold it in place.

◎

Wire matching bought beads onto head pins and insert between calottes (instead of jump rings).

A BOX FULL OF COLORFUL EMBROIDERY THREADS inspired this unique bracelet. It is a wonderful way to use up thread left over from other projects. The design can be worked in endless color combinations, from the soft and subtle to contrasting, bright colors. The basic idea can be used in lots of other ways by varying the finding and what it is securing. For example, to change the look of this project the threads could be braided, woven, or knotted and even swapped with ribbons, fabrics, piping cord, fancy knitting yarns, or almost anything you can secure successfully in the finding. The findings themselves can be varied, too. Watch for different styles of crimps, especially those recommended for use with thicker threads, such as leather thong.

3 or 4 skeins of
cotton embroidery thread
Scissors
14 square calotte crimps
Clear-drying, all-purpose craft glue
Round- and needle-nosed pliers
8 jump rings
Clasp

Getting Started

Obtain about 14 square calotte crimps—the total number that you need will depend on your wrist measurement and the length of each thread link. To keep the threads taut as you twist them together, tie them to a door knob.

75

HARLEQUIN THREADS

1. Select the colors you want to incorporate in the link—the links can be all the same or each link can be worked with different color combinations.

2. Cut each thread to a length of approximately 18 inches / 46 cm, smooth them out, and lay them side by side.

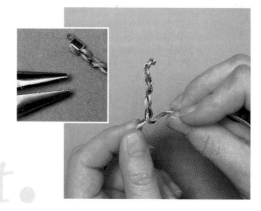

3. Hold the threads tightly at one end or tie them to a door knob. Twist them together, working in the same direction all the time, until they are so tight they begin to buckle.

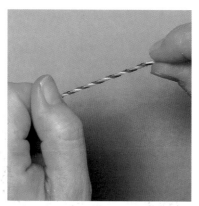

4. Fold the length of thread in half and let it twist around itself to form a cord. Working from the fold, insert the end of the cord into a square calotte crimp. Add a tiny blob of glue to the calotte before inserting the cord for added security. Use needle- or flat-nosed pliers to fold the edges of the crimp over the thread securely.

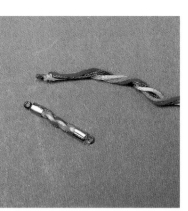

5

Keeping the cord tightly twisted, place another square calotte crimp approximately 1 inch / 2.5 cm farther along the cord and secure as before. Keep the calotte seams facing in the same direction. Trim threads below the loop of each calotte with the tips of a sharp pair of scissors.

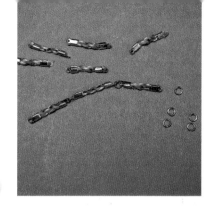

6

Using pliers, twist open the jump rings and slip them through the loops on 2 calottes to join them together. Twist the ends of the rings back together to close.

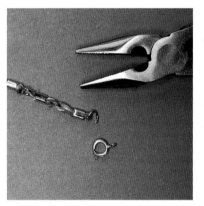

Join enough links to form a bracelet to fit comfortably around your wrist without falling off. Open up a jump ring and slip it through both the loop on a bolt ring clasp and the loop on the last calotte. Close to secure. Add a jump ring to the loop on the last calotte at the opposite end.

Variations on a Theme

Twisted paper giftwrap cord is cut into individual lengths, knotted, and made into a linked bracelet using square calotte crimps (right).

The velvet-covered piping cord shown here is just a single example of the different materials you can use to make this style of bracelet (far right).

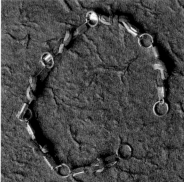

Hellenic
KEYS

Design Tips

Experiment with different cardboard shapes—start with a solid outline and then divide it into segments.

Trim the outer edges of each segment with shaped craft scissors for a different look, or simply cut an evenly pointed edge.

Experiment with jeweler's wire and pliers to make your own spirals and coils for joining the segments together.

Have fun playing with different decorative ideas; experiment with unusual materials like the copper and candy wrapper foil used for the variations here.

Substitute the cardboard with balsa wood, which is easy to cut with a heavy duty craft knife or hand saw.

THIS TURQUOISE AND GOLD BRACELET is made from thick cardboard that has been hand-painted and brushed with a couple of coats of PVA glue. The glue dries to a clear shiny finish, like varnish, protecting the surface of the design and giving the cardboard a little flexibility. The central motif is based on the traditional Greek "Key" design discovered in a book on ancient civilizations. Remember that when looking for ideas for designs or decoration, it is important to study things that are not always obvious. Looking only at different styles of jewelry designs in museums, fashion magazines, or galleries will not necessarily produce fresh ideas, but a closer look at the motifs decorating a Phoenician carving or Roman urn might. Stiff cardboard painted with PVA will last quite a while, but the shapes could also be papier-mâchéd for greater longevity.

Getting Started

Measure your wrist with a length of thread and decide where you would like the bracelet to finish. You may find it helpful to first draw an oblong approximately 1½ inches / 3.8 cm wide by the finished length, then contour the edges, taking them inside the oblong rather than outside.

You Will Need

Thick cardboard
Pencil
Ruler
Craft knife
Fine pointed bradawl
Gold and turquoise paints
Paintbrush
Metallic gold marker pen
PVA glue
Approximately 10 jump rings
Pliers
Clasp

HELLENIC KEYS

1. Draw your cardboard shape out to the measurement obtained by wrapping thread around your wrist.

2. Using a pencil and ruler, divide the shape into sections of equal width. Cut out the shape cleanly, using a craft knife and ruler. Trim any frayed edges with sharp scissors.

3. Place the shape back together again and mark 4 holes on each piece, taking care to align them all. Pierce the cardboard with a bradawl.

4. Outline a border on each cardboard piece that echoes the contoured edges. Paint it gold and let it dry.

Fill in the center with turquoise paint, adding a second coat if necessary. Let it dry.

Draw the center motif, using a gold metallic marker pen. Let it dry and then paint both sides with 1 or 2 coats of PVA glue.

Lay the decorated cardboard shapes out in the right order, twist open the jump rings using pliers, and use them to link the cardboard sections together. Twist each jump ring back to close it securely.

Variations on a Theme

The curved sections of this bracelet are decorated with motifs cut from sheet copper, then linked together with copper coils made by winding copper wire around pliers (right).

This bracelet can be made from cardboard cut into squares. Each section is painted black, decorated with a green foil motif, and linked together with green elastic cord (far right).

Experiment by working the same pattern with different-sized beads.

◉

The simple flower shape can also be worked in stunning color combinations like yellow and electric blue or red and orange. For more traditional flowers, combine white beads with yellow centers, or orange beads with black centers.

◉

Books on more complex bead-weaving patterns are a great source of inspiration for both color combinations and patterns.

◉

To make your own bead designs, paint small wooden beads using hobby enamels or artist's acrylic paint.

Daisy
CHAINS

THIS SIMPLE IDEA FOR A CHAIN OF FLOWERS IS easy to work and can be completely transformed by using different-sized beads and colors. Ideally the beads you choose should be smooth, like glass rocailles. This design is one of the easiest to master. If you are looking for more inspiration, look at illustrated books featuring the works of African tribal artisans or Native Americans. Or find a sourcebook on Victorian jewelry.

You Will Need

Black glass beads
Silver beads
Strong cotton thread or nylon line
Needle
2 calotte crimps
Clasp

Getting Started

Cut two lengths of thread to the required finished length for your wrist plus 8 inches / 20 cm for knotting and threading. Obtain as many black glass beads and silver beads as you will need to make 6 or 7 flower shapes on the bracelet.

DAISY CHAINS

1. Knot the ends of the threads together and secure the knot in the cup of a calotte crimp.

2. Begin the design by threading on 3 silver beads.

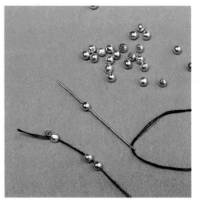

3. Next, add 4 black beads.

4. Add a silver bead (this will be the center bead).

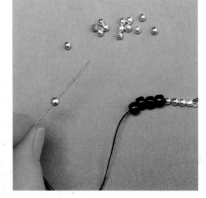

5. Take the needle back through the first black bead.

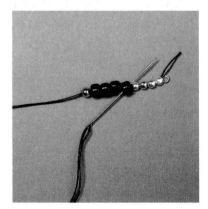

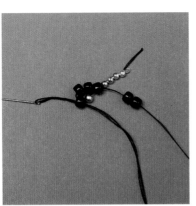

6. Add 2 more black beads and take the needle through the fourth bead. Draw the thread up carefully and push the beads into shape.

7. Add 3 silver beads before working the next flower.

8. When you have worked as many flowers as you need, finish with 3 silver beads and knot the thread close to the last bead. Enclose the knot in a calotte crimp, attach a clasp and jump ring to one end, and a single jump ring to the other end to complete the design.

Variations on a Theme

Larger beads in different colors give the same flower design a completely different look (right).

For a more delicate effect, weave tiny metallic beads in the same pattern (far right).

Cotton
CANDIES

Design Tips

Practice different color schemes on
a piece of paper first. Paint a layer
of nail polish, then add watercolors.
This will give you some idea of
how much paint you need to load
on to your brush and also which
colors work best together.

After you have worked out the colors
you want to use, paint a few practice
beads, making a note of the order of
the colors so the next bead can be
made in the same way.

Experiment using different-sized
balls or same-sized balls,
or mixing them together.

Paint each bead in a different
color combination on the same
nail polish base.

Metal coils or spirals can be
substituted for the figure-eight links.
They are easy to make by wrapping
the wire around pliers.

THESE BEADS LOOK LIKE fired ceramic but are actually made from simple pressed cotton balls that are used for making doll's heads. The eye-catching marbled effect is easy to achieve by painting them with nail polish and watercolor paints. The paints sit on top of the varnish, making it easy to merge the colors together. It may look complicated, but all it takes is a little practice and the end result is an expensive-looking bracelet.

Getting Started

Figure-eight links are easy to make from jeweler's wire if you use pliers to fashion the loops. Make sure the ends meet in the center or they will slip off the head pins—a tiny blob of clear-drying glue will help. Test the metallic pen on paper before applying to the bead; if the nib is loaded with too much color, it will smudge.

You Will Need

7 or 8 small pressed cotton balls
Toothpicks
Nail polish (1 colored and 1 neutral)
Watercolor paints
Piece of foam or plasticine
to support beads for drying
Metallic pen
Jeweler's wire
Wire cutters
Pliers
Head pins

COTTON CANDIES

1.

Use toothpicks to pierce through each ball—they usually have only partly drilled holes. Push the toothpick back into the bead from the opposite end, pushing back inside any protruding cotton.

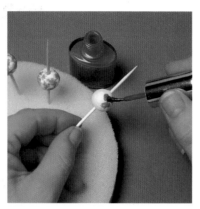

2.

a) Begin the marbling effect by stippling each ball with colored nail polish—don't cover it completely. b) Build up the color with white, then pale pink water-color splotches, and let dry. c) Coat each ball completely with neutral varnish. d) When dry, add more white splotches and immediately add the light red, just drawing the tip of the paintbrush into the white. Let it dry and coat with neutral varnish again. Repeat (d), adding more colors if required until you are happy with the finish.

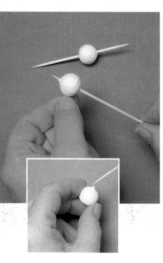

3.

Use the metallic pen to add highlights randomly over the bead.

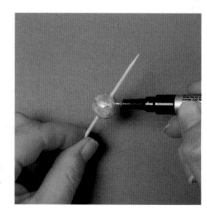

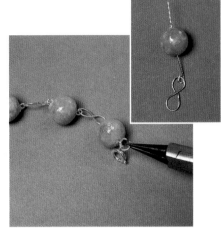

Cut a length of jeweler's wire to make the figure-eight links. With the end of the wire held between the fingers of the pliers, wrap the wire over the pliers and bring back to the center point. Slip the loop off the pliers and hold the

wire again at the center point as shown. Work the second loop in the opposite direction, bringing the wire back to the center point. Release from the pliers and trim excess wire with cutters at the center point.

Snip the "head" off the head pins and start to turn a loop at an end. Before completing the loop, slip an end of a metal link into it and then close the loop. Push the pin through the center of a marbled bead and repeat the process at the other side. Join enough beads and links to form a bracelet that fits around your wrist without falling off. Open up a jump ring and slip it through both the loop on a bolt ring clasp and the loop on the last bead. Close to secure. Add a jump ring to the loop on the last bead at the opposite end.

Variations on a Theme

Blue and purple watercolor paints merge together on top of a coat of nail polish to create this marbled effect. The beads are strung with silver metal coils made by wrapping jeweler's wire around a pencil (right).

Experiment with different colors and build up the design in layers, letting the paints dry before marbling the next set of colors (far right).

Acknowledgments

Grateful thanks to the many people without whose help and support this book would not have been published. First and most important, to my parents for their endless patience and for turning a blind eye when I used their home as a design studio. To Lindsey Stock and Jackie Schou for their additional design ideas, and to Paul Forrester for his creative photography. And, finally, to Shawna Mullen and Martha Wetherill, who made sense of everything I have written and gave valuable support and encouragement when times got tough.

About the Author

Jo Moody is a journalist who specializes in fashion and craft, and who has spent many years working for women's magazines. She is now a freelance stylist and writer, contributing features and designs to a variety of publications.

Her childhood fascination with jewelry has developed into a passion—she loves rediscovering traditional crafts and using them in new ways to transform everyday things into truly beautiful jewelry.

index

Sketch your ideas...

Jo.
bracelets